John Milner, Pope Pius VII

Bishop Milner's Devotion to the Sacred Heart of Jesus

with the indult of his Holiness Pope Pius VII in favour of that devotion

John Milner, Pope Pius VII

Bishop Milner's Devotion to the Sacred Heart of Jesus
with the indult of his Holiness Pope Pius VII in favour of that devotion

ISBN/EAN: 9783337104221

Printed in Europe, USA, Canada, Australia, Japan

Cover: Foto ©Lupo / pixelio.de

More available books at **www.hansebooks.com**

"I will speak to His Heart, and obtain from
it whatever I desire."

St. Bonaventure,
In Stimulo Amoris, Part I, Cap. I.

R. *Washbourne*, 13, *Paternoster Row, London.*

BISHOP MILNER'S DEVOTION

TO THE

Sacred Heart of Jesus:

WITH THE INDULT OF

HIS HOLINESS POPE PIUS VII.

IN FAVOUR OF THAT DEVOTION.

NEW EDITION:

TO WHICH IS ADDED

DEVOTIONS TO THE IMMACULATE HEART OF MARY.

LONDON:

ROBERT B. WASHBOURNE,

13, PATERNOSTER ROW.

1867.

I _____

was received into the Society of the Sacred Heart of

Jesus on _____ 18____

at _____

by _____

I ____   _____

was received into the Society of the Immaculate Heart

of Mary on _____ 18____

THE FAITHFUL

OF

THE MIDLAND DISTRICT.

Dearly beloved Brethren and Children in Jesus Christ,

AS it is our first and indispensable duty to keep God's commandments —"If thou wilt enter into life," says Christ, "keep the commandments" (Matt. xix, 17)—so it ought to be our primary and chief devotion, to worship God by the exercises of faith, hope, and charity. Still it has been the general practice of the saints and other eminent servants of God to unite with the exercise of these divine virtues, as a means of nourishing and increasing them, certain particular devotions, according as they have been inspired by the Holy Ghost, or prompted by their own reflections. Some of these holy personages have devoted themselves to the special service of that most pure and holy of creatures by means of whom our Redeemer Jesus Christ was given to us ; others have dedicated their lives to the perpetual adoration of this incarnate God, in the adorable Sacrament of the Altar ; others have consecrated themselves to the particular worship of the precious wounds, or the venerable countenance, or the loving Heart of the divine Jesus. The last-mentioned devotion having for its ultimate object the infinite love which induced the Son of God to do and to suffer what he has done and suffered for us, namely, to give himself to be our companion in his incarnation, our food in his divine Sacrament, and our bleeding victim in his bitter passion, has been particularly cherished and practised by the saints and other distinguished servants of God in these latter ages, in which " iniquity hath abounded and the charity of many hath grown cold " (Matt. xxiv. 12). Hence, also, it has been more plentifully enriched with the spiritual treasures of the Church.

If we would trace the devotion to the Sacred Heart of Jesus to its true source, it may be said to have issued, together with the last drop of his blood, from the wound inflicted on it by the soldier's spear, at the moment of his death on the cross: for such is the doctrine of the saints who have treated of this matter. The inflamed St. Augustin says: " The lance has opened the side of Jesus to me ; I have entered into it, and there have I dwelt as in a secure refuge " (Manuale, c. 23). The devout St. Bernard enlarges on this sentiment as follows : " The side of the Lord was opened that we might be enabled to enter into it :—Yes, for this reason, O blessed Jesus, was thy heart wounded, that, being free from all exterior disturbances, we may repose in it. O how good and how sweet is it to make our abode in this heart ! O most amiable Jesus, how rich a treasure, how inestimable a pearl, is thy Sacred Heart ! I will cheerfully give up all that I have in order to possess it. It is in this temple and sanctuary, and before this ark of the testament, that I will adore and bless the name of the Lord, saying with the prophet : ' Thy servant hath found his heart, to pray this prayer to thee ' (2 Kings vii, 27); and I have found the Heart of Jesus, my king, my brother, and my friend; and, having found this Heart, what can I do but adore it !—Draw me entirely into this Sacred Heart, that I may dwell in it all the days of my life.—O thou most beautiful of the children of men, thy side was opened for no other end but to give us an entrance to thy Heart; and this Heart itself was not opened but to afford us a dwelling free from all things that can disturb our repose. This adorable Heart was pierced, that, through its visible wound, we might see and understand the invisible wound which his love of us had inflicted on it. O, how could Jesus testify his love of us more strongly than by resolving that not only his body but also his very Heart should be pierced for us ! Who, then, can help loving a Heart thus wounded ! Who

can be insensible to so much love!"
(Tract de Passion.) The same doctrine
is taught by the Angelic Doctor, St.
Thomas, where he says: "Christ poured
forth the blood of his side and Heart to
warm and vivify his disciples and others
who are weak and tempted in their
faith, and therefore cold, and, as it
were, dead" (Opusc. 58). His seraphi-
cal contemporary, St. Bonaventure, inflamed with the same devout idea, thus
exclaims: "O amiable wounds, thro'
which I have entered and penetrated
to the very entrails of the charity of
Jesus Christ!—Henceforward I will
never be separated from him, because
it is good to be with him, and in him I
will make three tabernacles, one in his
hands, one in his feet, and another,
which I will never quit, in his sacred
side: there I will speak to his Heart,
and obtain from it whatever I stand in
need of. Thus I shall tread in the steps
of his beloved Mother, whose soul was
pierced through with the sword of her
blessed Son's passion" (Stim. Amor).
How many passages in the enlightened

writings of that great master of a
spiritual life, St. Francis of Sales, are
embalmed with his devotion to the
Sacred Heart! In one of these he cries
out: "O love, O sovereign love of the
Heart of Jesus! what heart can bless
and praise thee as thou deservest to be
blessed and praised!" In another
passage he invites pious souls to the
practice of this devotion, saying: "How
good and bountiful is the Lord Jesus!
how perfect and amiable is his Heart!
Let this amiable Heart ever live in our
hearts."

It would swell this treatise to a dis-
proportionate size were I to quote the
several testimonies and sentiments of
St. Peter Damian, St. Gertrude, St.
Mechtildes, St. Catharine of Sienna,
the devout Blosius, and other saints
and pious writers in behalf of this devotion; still less can we here enumerate
the States and Dioceses in the four
parts of the world in which it has been
sanctioned and propagated by due ec-
clesiastical authority, and by that of
the Holy See in particular, which has

issued a number of Decrees to this effect.*

* The Decretum POLONA, issued under Clement XIII. in 1785, testifies as follows : " Cultum CORDIS JESU jam hodie esse per omnes fere Catholici orbis partes, faventibus eorum episcopis, propagatum ; sæpe etiam à Sede Apostolicâ donatum millenis Indulgentiarum Brevibus."

N.B. The following censures of Pope Pius VI. in his condemnation of the Synod of Pistoja (which condemnation is received as a rule of faith by the whole Church), on certain propositions of that Synod, deserve to be here cited in confirmation of the devotion in question, and as explaining its nature.

LXI. "Propositio quæ asserit, *adorare directe Humanitatum Christi, magis vero aliquam ejus partem, fore semper honorem divinum dare creaturæ :—* Quatenus per hoc verbum *directe* intendat reprobare adorationis cultum, quem Fideles dirigunt ad Humanitatem Christi, perinde ac si talis adoratio, quâ Humanitás, ipsaque caro vivifica Christi adoratur, non quidem propter se, et tanquam nuda caro, sed prout unita Divinitati, foret *honor divinus impetitus creaturæ,* et non potius *una eademque adoratio, qua Verbum Incarnatum cum propriá ipsius carne adoratur : —Falsa, captiosa, pio ac debito cultui Humanitati Christi à Fidelibus præstito ac præstando, detrahens, et injuriosa.*"

LXII. "Doctrina, quæ devotionem erga Sacratissimum COR JESU *rejecit inter devotiones, quas notat velut novas, erroneas, aut saltem periculosas :—*Intellecta de hac devotione qualis est ab Apostolicâ Sede probata :——*Falsa, temeraria, perniciosa, piarum aurium offensiva, in Apostolicam Sedem injuriosa.*"

LXIII. " Item in eo quod cultores CORDIS JESU

From what has been here said and quoted, it will be gathered that the object of this devotion is not the material Heart of our blessed Saviour; but the same, as it constitutes a most noble and essential part of his humanity ; as it is the peculiar seat of his immense charity; and as it is hypostatically united with the Divinity itself. In fact, it is the incomprehensible, infinite love of this incarnate God for us poor mortals, which made him " obedient unto death, even the death of the cross," and which still detains him our willing captive and victim in the adorable Sacrifice of the Altar, that is the principal object of this devotion ;* as, indeed, its

hoc etiam nomine arguit, quod *non advertant Sanctissimam Carnem Christi, aut ejus partem aliquam, aut etiam Humanitatem totam cum separatione aut præcisione à Divinitate adorari non posse cultu latriæ :*
——Quasi Fideles COR JESU adorarent cum separatione vel præcisione à Divinitate, cum illud adorant, ut est COR JESU, *cor nempe Personæ Verbi, cui inseparabiliter unitum est,* ad eum modum quo exsangue Corpus Christi in triduo mortis sine separatioue aut præcisione à Divinitate adorabile fuit in sepulchro :
——*Captiosa, in Fideles* CORDIS CHRISTI *cultores injuriosa.*"

* " Cultus Sacri Cordis non consistit *in corde ipso*

ultimate end is to inflame our hearts with a reciprocal love for this most amiable and loving Redeemer, conformably with the first injunction of his *great commandment* of love, " Thou shalt love the Lord thy God with all thy heart " (Matt. xxiii, 37) ; and in compliance with the earnest desire which he testifies where he says : " I am come to cast fire on the earth ; and what do I desire but that it be enkindled " (Luke xii. 49).

This devotion to the Sacred Heart of Jesus may be practised either singly and in private, or in a sodality or assembly, held for this purpose. All that is required on the part of the faithful of the Midland District, who wish to avail themselves of the first of the following grants of his Holiness, made in their favour, is, that, having confessed their sins with true contrition, and received the blessed Eucharist, they visit some public chapel or private oratory,

nudo et solitarie sumpto sed *in corde Jesu humanitati sacro-sanctæ, sive divino corpori unito,* et consequenter *rem unam cum anima et divina persona constituente.*" Bened. XIV. De Canoniz. c. Sanct. L. iv. 31,

where a representation of the *Most Holy Heart of Jesus* is exhibited, some time between the first vespers or afternoon before *the Festival of the Sacred Heart,** and the sun-setting of the festival itself, or on the Sunday following that festival; and, in like manner, on the afternoon preceding the first Friday or Sunday of every month, and the sun-setting of the day itself, at the discretion of their authorized pastor, and there shall pray for peace and concord among Christian princes, the extirpation of heresies, and the other pious intentions of his Holiness. In return, such persons will, on each of the above-mentioned occasions, gain a Plenary Indulgence, which is applicable, by way of suffrage, to the souls of the faithful departed. The second grant of his Holiness to the

---

* The Festival of *The Sacred Heart of Jesus* was instituted in consequence of a revelation of our Blessed Saviour to St. Mary Margaret Alacoque, about the middle of the seventeenth century. This revelation resembled, in most of its circumstances, that made to the blessed Juliana, a religious of the thirteenth century, which revelation occasioned the institution of the Festival of *Corpus Christi.*

faithful of the said district, is that of an Indulgence of one hundred days, in like manner applicable, by way of suffrage, to the faithful departed, once every day, to each of them who shall devoutly visit the aforesaid representation, and shall then pray for the above-mentioned ends.

Nevertheless, as social worship is, generally speaking, preferable, on many accounts, to private worship, we cannot but approve of such associations in honour of THE SACRED HEART, as the several Pastors of the Midland District shall find it practicable and expedient to form in their respective congregations. We are far, however, from wishing that the exercises of this devotion should interfere with the regular service of the Church, or the sermons, lectures, or catechetical instructions, so necessary for the faithful in general, or with the prayers, examination of conscience, and other pious practices now in use; neither would we have these late Indulgences to supersede or to interfere with the eight general Indulgences granted to the Catholics of

England in the course of the year. In short, we do not think it generally advisable to form whole congregations into Societies of the Sacred Heart, but rather to confine the latter to certain pious and edifying persons of each flock, whom their Pastors shall judge most likely to improve in their love and fidelity to our most amiable and loving Saviour, by the practice of this devotion; and we hereby leave it to the discretion of each established Pastor, to appoint the Fridays .or the Sundays above-mentioned for gaining the specified Indulgences by the faithful of their respective congregations.——It follows from what has been said, that when families or individuals live at a distance from the chapel or other place where the sodality is accustomed to meet, or are otherwise prevented from attending it, they may gain the above-mentioned Indulgences, by placing a representation of the Sacred Heart in their own private oratories, and there performing their devotions in the manner that has been described.

We here subjoin a collection of pious prayers and exercises of devotion to the SACRED HEART OF JESUS, adapted both to public sodalities and private devotion, many of which are borrowed from other approved works.

✠ JOHN BP. OF CASTABALA, V.A. M.D.

——o——

An Act of Consecration to the Sacred Heart of Jesus.

O MY most amiable and loving God, who callest upon me to " give thee my heart " (Prov. xxiii, 26), and commandest me "to love thee with my whole heart " (Matt. xxii. 27), I most earnestly desire to perform this duty ; " for what have I in heaven ; and besides thee, what do I desire upon earth ? For thee my flesh and my heart have fainted away : thou the God of my heart, and the God that art my portion for ever " (Ps. lxxii, 24). Thou art the source of all perfection and all being, whom " the angels delight to behold " (1 Pet. i, 12). Thou hast thought of me in thy love and bounty from all eternity, and hast bestowed upon me in time this excellent being, " a little inferior to the angels" (Ps. viii. 6), that I possess, and thou dost support me every instant of my existence, to prevent my falling back into my original nothingness. When I was lost in sin, and had become the destined victim of hell's unquenchable flames, thou, the co-equal Son of the Eternal Father," according to the riches of thy grace (Ephes. i, 7), and thy super-abundant love for me, didst offer thyself an atoning victim to the justice of thy Father, taking upon thee my imperfect nature, in order to suffer in my stead. And, O my loving Redeemer, what dreadful ignominies and torments hast thou not suffered for this purpose? What deadly anguish oppressed thee in the Garden of Gethsemani! What unparalleled insults and torments didst thou endure from the Jews and Pagan soldiers! What more than mortal pangs convulsed thy body and soul, whilst thou pouredst out thy precious blood on the cross, derided by thy enemies, and forsaken by thy heavenly Father! O thou, my too loving and bountiful Saviour, is it possible that this excess of thy love for me should not engage me to love thee in return! No, sweet Jesus, I will and do "love thee, because thou hast loved me first" (1 John iv, 19). I will and do love thee, as thou commandest me, "with my whole heart, with my whole soul, and with my whole mind" (Matt. xxii, 37). Trusting in thy all-powerful grace, I resolve, with thy Apostle, that henceforth "neither tribulation, nor distress, nor famine, nor nakedness, nor danger, nor persecution, nor the sword, shall be able to separate me from the love of God, which is in Christ Jesus our Lord" (Rom. viii, 35). But, in order that I may thus love thee, divest me, O my divine Master, of the inordinate love which I bear to myself: enable me to "take up thy sweet yoke, and to learn of thee to be meek and humble of heart" (Matt. xi, 29). Penetrate my heart with a deep sense of its own misery and sinfulness, that "in humility I may esteem others better

than myself" (Phil. ii, 3). O thou meek
and humble Heart of my Jesus! O
thou most amiable Heart, ever glowing
with love for me, frame my heart to
resemble thine. Teach me to know
myself, by a deep conviction of my own
unworthiness : teach me to know thee,
by an ardent love of thee, that henceforward thou mayest be the moving
principle of my heart, in all that I shall
think, and say, and do, during the re-
mainder of this mortal life, till it comes
to be absorbed in the abyss of pure
love for all eternity, *Amen.*

V. *Thy loving Heart, O Jesus, I adore:*
R. *With love my heart inflame still
     more and more.*

———o———

*An Act of Atonement to the Sacred
Heart of Jesus.*

O ADORABLE JESUS! how insensible
     are the hearts of men, how insen-
sible is my heart in particular, of the
infinite love of us, with which thy Sacred
Heart is inflamed! The blessed spirits
celebrated the mysteries of thy incar-

nation and birth; they ministered to thee in the agony that preceded thy passion, and at thy resurrection from the dead; they surround our altars, to adore thy real presence upon them; yet how little impression do these mysteries make upon our frozen hearts, for the love of whom they have all been wrought! How feeble is our faith in them! how tepid is our gratitude for them! how little love or respect do we prove to thee in the most holy Sacrament of the Altar, in which, nevertheless, thou art as truly present as thou wert upon the cross on Mount Calvary and as thou wilt be in the clouds of heaven at the last day, when thou wilt pronounce our everlasting doom! But we are not only insensible, we are perfidious and rebellious. How grievously do we transgress thy holy commands by wilful sin! how unconcernedly do we "drink down iniquity like water" (Job xv, 16)! How frequently have I myself, like the traitor Judas, betrayed thee into the hands of thy enemies and my own for some unlawful gratification!

how have I even " trodden under foot
the Son of God, and esteemed the
blood of the testament unclean, by
which I was sanctified " (Heb. x. 29),
by abusing the institutions of his mercy,
for conveying the merits of his precious
sufferings to my soul! O the base return of my unfeeling heart, to the unparalleled mercy and love of the most
tender and generous Heart of my Saviour! Would to God that I were able,
with never-ceasing tears, and the last
drop of my blood, to atone for so much
guilt and ingratitude! But, since no
created being can make due satisfaction
to the offended majesty of God, I here
offer him the divine ardours of the Heart
of his Son Jesus Christ, to satisfy for
the ingratitude of mine ; and I present
to him the blood that flowed from his
wounded Heart, at his last gasp on the
cross, in satisfaction for my own sins,
and those of my fellow-creatures ; earnestly beseeching thee, my God, rather
to take me out of the world at the present moment, than let me live to offend
thee grievously any more. *Amen.*

V. *Thy loving Heart, O Jesus, I adore :*

R. *With love my heart inflame still more and more.*

————o————

Devout Salutations to the Sacred Humanity of Jesus Christ.

ETERNAL Son of the living God, who, in the excess of thy mercy and love, didst take upon thee our human nature, to suffer in it the punishment due to my sins, what grateful homage and love do I not owe to this sacred humanity, sacrificed wholly and in each part for my salvation!—I salute thee then, O precious body of Christ, suffering cold and want at thy birth — hunger and fatigue during thy life— and a bloody scourging, which rendered thee " like a leper, and as one struck by God " (Isa. liii, 4), before thy death.

R. *I salute and adore thee, thou dear suffering body of my Lord and Redeemer Jesus Christ.*

Prostrate before you, I salute and adore you, O sacred feet of my Redeemer, so often wearied, during his mortal course, in "seeking the lost sheep of the house of Israel" (Matt. xv, 24), and at length transfixed with torturing nails to the wood of the cross.

R. *I salute and adore you, O bleeding feet of my Saviour Jesus Christ.*

I salute and adore you, omnipotent hands of my gracious Master, which healed the sick, and wrought other miracles for his people, and, in return, were nailed by them to the instrument of his torture, in order to exhaust his life by lengthened sufferings.

R. *I salute and adore you, O bountiful hands of my Saviour Jesus Christ, bleeding on the cross.*

I salute and adore you, O venerable head and countenance of the Word Incarnate, on which the angels look with awe, but which by his sinful creatures were buffeted, and blindfolded, and spit upon, and crowned with thorns.

R. *I salute and adore thee, O divine countenance of my awful Judge, and I beseech thee, that, instead of thy terrible frown, I may meet with thy gracious smile, when thou shalt unveil thyself to me.*

I salute and adore thee, O sacred spirit of the divine Jesus, which, from the moment of his conception, foresaw and accepted of all the ignominies and pains he successively endured ; oppressed with sorrow even unto death, in the Garden of Gethsemani, and left by the Eternal Father to the extremity of interior and exterior torment, till their violence exhausted and took away his breath.

R. *I salute and adore thee, O most afflicted spirit of my willing victim Jesus Christ, and beg of thee that I may henceforward love him with all my soul and all my mind.*

I salute and adore thee, O glowing heart of my best friend Jesus Christ, that wert laid open at his death, to give me, with the last drop of his life's blood, the final proof of his boundless love for me.

R. *I salute and adore thee, O precious Heart of Jesus, that loved me unto death : grant that I may love thee with all my heart now and for evermore.* Amen.

————o————

The short LITANY *of the* SACRED HEART.

LORD, have mercy on us.
　　R. *Lord, have mercy on us.*
Christ, have mercy on us.
　　R. *Christ, have mercy on us.*
Lord, have mercy on us.
　　R. *Lord, have mercy on us.*
Christ, hear us.
　　R. *Christ, graciously hear us.*
O God, the Father of our Lord Jesus Christ, *Have mercy on us.*
O God the Son, the Redeemer of mankind, *Have mercy on us.*
O God the Holy Ghost, the Comforter of the just, *Have mercy on us.*
O Sacred Trinity, three Persons in one God, *Have mercy on us.*
Sacred Heart of Jesus.
　　R. *Grant us grace to love thee.*

Sacred Heart of Jesus, hypostatically
  united with the Eternal Word,

Sacred Heart of Jesus, furnace of divine love,

Sacred Heart of Jesus, mirror of
  meekness and humility,

Sacred Heart of Jesus, source of
  true contrition,

Sacred Heart of Jesus, the treasury
  of all graces,

Sacred Heart of Jesus, *sorrowful in
  the Garden unto death,*

Sacred Heart of Jesus, fainting under
  his bloody sweat,

Sacred Heart of Jesus, *saturated with
  affronts,* (Lament. iii. 30.)

Sacred Heart of Jesus, *obedient unto
  the death of the cross,* (Phillip. ii. 8.)

Sacred Heart of Jesus, pierced with
  the soldier's spear,

Sacred Heart of Jesus, the refuge of
  sinners,

Sacred Heart of Jesus, the consola-
  tion of the afflicted,

Sacred Heart of Jesus, the hope of
  the dying,

Grant us grace to love thee.—

Sacred Heart of Jesus, the joy of the elect, R. *Grant us grace to love thee.*
From insensibility of thy infinite love for us, *Deliver us, O Heart of Jesus.*
From the ingratitude of wilfully offending thee, *Deliver us, O Heart of Jesus.*
From the misery of being separated from thee in time and eternity, *Deliver us, O Heart of Jesus.*

V. O Jesus, meek and humble of heart.

R. O Jesus, make our hearts like unto thy heart.

Let us pray.

O JESUS CHRIST, who, from the full treasury of thy Sacred Heart, didst draw the inestimable graces which thou dispensest to thy faithful lovers, grant that, mortifying our pride and self-love, we may become true imitators of thy meekness and humility, and becoming every day more sensible of thy excessive love, in making thyself our companion in thy Incarnation, our victim in thy Passion and Death, and our food in thy Real Presence on our altars, we may henceforward return thee, to the best of our power, love for love during this our present state, and be immersed hereafter in the abyss of thy divine love, who with the Father and the Holy Ghost livest and reignest one God, world without end. *Amen.*

———o———

A Prayer proper for gaining the Indulgences granted by his Holiness.

O MOST just and merciful God, my Father, my Redeemer, my Sanctifier, my God, and my All! when I reflect on my insensibility of thy numberless and incomprehensible benefits towards me, the tepidity of my services to thee, my daily transgressions against thee, and more especially on the great sins of my past life, and on the imperfection of my contrition and penance for them, I am seized with grief and terror, and wish with thy prophet, for "water to my head, and a fountain of tears to my eyes, that day and night I may bewail (Jerem. ix) my guilt and

misery. Hence also I cry out to thee
with another of thy prophets :—

Have mercy on me, O God, according
to thy great mercy.

R. *And according to the multitude of
thy tender mercies, blot out my sins.*

Wash me yet more from my iniquity,
and cleanse me from my sin.

R. *For I know my iniquity, and my
sin is always before me.*

To thee only have I sinned, and have
done evil before thee (Ps. l).

Nevertheless, assured as I am, O Lord,
that thy "mercies are above all thy
works" (Ps. xl), and that thou, my loving
Saviour, didst suffer the torments of the
cross, and give thy Heart's blood to
make an atonement for me, I cast myself with an humble hope at thy cruci-
fied feet, and beseech thee to apply this
sovereign atonement to my poor soul.
" O sprinkle me with this hyssop [that
distils from thy precious wounds], and
I shall be cleansed; wash me [with
thy atoning blood], and I shall be made

whiter than snow " (Ps. 1). Yes, my most merciful Lord and Saviour, trusting, as I do, in the multitude of thy mercies, and the infinite merits of thy sufferings and death for me, as likewise in the prayers of the Blessed Virgin and all the saints, and in the virtue of the heavenly keys thou hast bestowed on thy Vicar on earth, I hope not only for the pardon of my sins, but also for the remission of the temporal punishments due to them ; and therefore, in compliance with the directions of this thy Vicar, I pray to thee most earnestly for the accomplishment of all his pious intentions, and more especially for the establishment of peace and concord among Christian princes and states, and for the extirpation of all heresies, schisms, infidelity, and wickedness throughout the world.—Grant all this, O Lord God, for thy mercy's sake, and through the sacred wounds and the pierced heart of thy beloved Son Jesus Christ, who with thee and the Holy Ghost lives and reigns one God, world without end. *Amen.*

*Our Father, &c.   Hail Mary, &c, I
believe in God, &c.*

———o———

A Condolence with the Sacred Heart of
the Blessed Virgin.

O Virgin Mother of my divine Redeemer Jesus Christ, how soon was
the joy that filled thy Heart at his birth,
allayed by the prophecy of holy Simeon,
announcing to thee at thy purification,
that "He was set up for a sign, that
should be contradicted, and that a
sword should transfix thy own soul"
(Luke xi. 34)! Accordingly thou didst
soon witness the cruel jealousy of King
Herod, who endeavoured to cut him off
at his birth, the blind fury of the people,
who took up stones, and led him to a
precipice in order to destroy him, and
the unwearied malice of the Scribes and
Pharisees, who sought for pretexts to
ruin his character, and put him to an
ignominious death; all which attempts
wounded thy tender Heart with a grief
proportionable to the fervour of thy
love of him, who was, at the same time

thy Son and thy God. But when, at length, in his merciful counsels for my salvation, he permitted a mortal anguish to overwhelm his soul, and his enemies to seize upon his divine person; when he was bound and buffeted, and blasphemed and spit upon; when he was torn with scourges and crowned with thorns, and sentenced to an ignominious death; when thy eyes beheld him fainting under the load of his cross, and hanging upon it for three hours supported by nails that transfixed his hands and feet, while the precious blood derived from thy pure body, streamed down from his several wounds; when thy ear heard his meek voice commending thee to his beloved disciple, and likewise his unrelenting enemies to the mercy of his heavenly Father, till the extremity of their torments took away his breath, O blessed Virgin Mother, how severe were thy pangs! how sharp was the sword that wounded thy maternal heart! Surely no sorrow of the afflicted was like unto thy sorrow! surely no sufferings of the martyrs in

their bodies were equal to the sufferings
thou didst endure in thy holy soul. I
condole with thee, thou most innocent,
and yet most afflicted of human beings,
and I bewail my sins, which have caused
thy divine Son's sufferings, and thy own
sorrows. Oh, by all thy love of him,
and compassion for me, I beseech thee
to obtain of him, that I may never more
deliberately offend him, but rather that
I may love him more and more every
day of my mortal life, till I come to the
clear sight and possession of him, in
company with thee and the other blessed
inhabitants of the kingdom of divine
love.   *Amen.*

V. *Great Queen of Sorrows, grant
that we may tread thy steps, and let it be
our sorrow not to grieve like thee.*

R. *O may the wounds of thy dear Son
    Our contrite hearts possess alone,
    And all terrene affections drown.*

————o————

A Prayer for a happy Death.

O ALMIGHTY and eternal God, the Creator of us, and of all things, who

didst create our bodies of the dust of the earth, and when we had sinned against thee, in our first father, didst sentence them to return to dust, behold I here submit to this awful sentence, as the just punishment of my sins, and as the only means of coming to thee, my last end and my supreme happiness. But, O my most merciful Lord and God, I beseech thee, through the passion and death of my Redeemer Jesus Christ, that, at whatever hour thou art pleased to summon me out of this world to the bar of thy justice in the next, I may be found watching with the lamp of faith, hope, and charity, burning in my hand, so as not to be shut out from the banquet of eternal happiness, but be admitted to the sight and enjoyment of thee in thy heavenly kingdom.

O JESUS, my most loving Saviour, who didst hang three hours on the cross to purchase mercy, grace, and salvation for my poor soul, I entreat thee, by thy precious wounds, and especially by that of thy adorable Heart,

c

which yielded the last drop of its sacred blood for me, that thou wouldst have mercy upon me at the hour of my death.

R. *Sacred Heart of Jesus, have mercy upon me at that my last hour.*

At that all-important hour, when my sentence for eternity is about to be pronounced, and my infernal enemies will redouble their efforts to get possession of my poor soul,

R. *Sacred Heart of Jesus, have mercy upon me at that my last hour.*

When my body, subdued by disease, and bedewed with a cold sweat, will be nearly motionless, and my mind, distracted with pain and anxiety, will be incapable of fixed attention or fervent prayer,

R. *Sacred Heart of Jesus, have mercy upon me at that my last hour.*

When I shall breathe forth my soul, and it shall behold thee on the throne of thy Majesty surrounded by millions of blessed spirits,

R. *Sacred Heart of Jesus, have mercy upon me at that my last hour.*

Let us pray for the Faithful departed.

OUT of the depths I have cried to thee, O Lord; Lord, hear my voice.

Let thy ears be attentive to the voice of my supplication.

If thou wilt observe iniquities, O Lord; Lord who shall endure it?

For with thee there is propitiation; and by reason of thy law I have waited for thee, O Lord.

My soul hath relied on his word. My soul hath hoped in the Lord.

From the morning watch even until night, let Israel hope in the Lord.

Because with the Lord there is mercy; and with him plentiful redemption.

And he shall redeem Israel from all his iniquities.

Eternal rest give to them, O Lord, and let perpetual light shine upon them.

Let us pray.

O GOD, the giver of pardon, and lover of the salvation of men, we beseech thy clemency in behalf of our parents, relations, friends, and benefactors, who have departed this life, that, the blessed Virgin Mary and all the saints interceding for them, they may come to the fellowship of eternal life, through Christ, our Lord.

O God, the Creator and Redeemer of all the faithful, give to the souls of thy servants departed the remission of all their sins, that through pious supplications they may obtain the pardon which they have always desired, who livest and reignest, world without end. *Amen.*

V. *Thy loving Heart, O Jesus, I adore:*
R. *With love my heart inflame still more and more.*

Sanctissimo Domino nostro Pio P. P. VII.

BEATISSIME PATER,

JOANNES MILNER, Dei et Apostolicæ Sedis gratiâ, Episcopus Castabalæ, Vicarius Apostolicus in Angliâ, ad Sanctitatis vestræ pedes provolutus humiliter supplicat, ut, ad augendum indies Amabilissimi Cordis Jesu Christi Domini nostri cultum, omnibus et singulis utriusque sexus Christi fidelibus, qui in locis suæ spiritualis jurisdictionis, in Feriâ Sextâ post Octavam Sanctissimi Corporis Christi, vel, loco ejusdem Feriæ, in unâ aliâ per annum die ab Oratore designandâ, nec non in primâ Sextâ Feriâ cujusque Mensis, vel, loco istiusmodi Feriarum, in unâ ex diebus Dominicis cujusque mensis, per Oratorem pariter assignandâ, vere pœnitentes et confessi ac sacrâ communione refecti, devote visitaverint, à primis vesperis usque ad occasum solis dierum hujusmodi, Imaginem Sanctissimi Cordis Jesu, vel expositam, vel quando exposita fuerit, in Ecclesiâ aut Sacello publico, sive Oratorio quocunque, etiam collocato intra septa cujuslibet Monasterii, Seminarii, vel alterius loci pii, et ibi pro Christianorum Principum concordiâ, hæresum extirpatione, ac juxta mentem Sanctitatis vestræ, preces effuderint, quâ die prædictarum id egerint, *Plenariam Indulgentiam,* applicabilem

etiam, per modum suffragii, animabus
fidelium defunctorum : iis vero, qui
indicatam Imaginem devote visitaverint, ibique, ut supra, oraverint, centum
dierum Indulgentiam in singulos anni
dies semel in die ab unoquoque lucran-
dam, pariterque, per modum suffragii,
applicandam, benigne concedere dig-
netur : quam gratiam, &c.

Ex Audientiâ Sanctissimi, die
27 Junii, 1814.

SANCTISSIMUS benigne annuit pro gratiâ juxta petita, in formâ tamen Ec-
clesiæ constitutâ, ad quindennium.

P. F. CARD. GALLEFI.

N.B. His Holiness Pope Pius VIII.
by a Rescript dated May 31, 1829, re-
newed the above Indulgences for fifteen
years more. Finally, Pope Gregory
XVI. granted the same in perpetuity.

The festival of the *Sacred Heart
of Jesus* is kept on the Sunday after
the Octave of Corpus Christi.

*Here end the Devotions published by
Bishop Milner.*

CHAPLET,

IN HONOUR OF THE SACRED HEART OF JESUS.

A Decree issued by the Congregation of Indulgences on the 20th March, 1815, and a Rescript of Pius VII. of the 26th September, 1817, grant to all the faithful who devoutly recite the little *Chaplet* in honour of the Sacred Heart of Jesus, the following indulgences :

"A *plenary Indulgence*, one day in each month at the choice of those who recite this Chaplet every day during the month.

" An *Indulgence of* 300 *days*, each time that the Chaplet is recited.

"Both applicable, by way of suffrage, to the souls in Purgatory."

This *Chaplet* is composed of five *Paternosters* and five *Gloria Patris*, with a versicle and prayer, as follows :

V. Incline unto my aid, O God !
R. O *Lord ! make haste to help me.*

I. O most amiable Jesus ! in beholding the compassion and mercy thou

entertainest for sinners, which shines
forth in thy divine Heart, I feel mine
bounding with joy, and filled with the
hope of being well received by thee.
Alas! how many sins have I committed:
but as, like repentant Peter and peni-
tent Magdalen, I deplore and detest
them, because they offend thee, O
Sovereign Good! grant unto me a
general pardon, and by thy tender
heart ordain that I may rather die
than offend thee, and that I may live
only to love thee.

Here are said one *Pater* and five
Glorias inhonour of the five wounds
and the divine Heart of Jesus, and then
the following aspiration:

O amiable Heart of Jesus! grant that
I may ever love thee more and more!

II. I bless, O Jesus! thy most humble Heart, and return thee thanks for
having given it as a model to mine.
Not only hast thou strongly incited me
to imitate it, but by it thou hast shewn
me and levelled for me the paths of
thy great humiliations. I have been
both ungrateful and insensible. Par-

don my wanderings. I will no longer
be the slave of pride or vanity, but
follow thee in the midst of humiliations,
with an humble heart, that I may obtain
peace and salvation; support me, and
I will bless thy Heart for all eternity.

One *Pater*, five *Glorias*—O amiable
Heart, &c.

III. I admire, O Jesus! thy most
patient Heart, and thank thee for the
wonderful examples of an invincible
meekness which thou hast left us. I
am afflicted at the sight of my extreme
delicacy, which cannot suffer the least
pain. Ah! Jesus, pour into my heart
a fervent and constant love of tribula-
tions, crosses, mortification and penance, to the end that, following thee to
Calvary, I may deserve to be united to
thee in the delights and the glory of
Paradise.

One *Pater*, five *Glorias*—O amiable
Heart, &c.

IV. In beholding the infinite meekness of thy Heart, O my Jesus! I have a

horror of mine, which is so different to thine. Alas! a shadow, a gesture, a word which is contrary to mine, suffices to afflict and to trouble me. Pardon these transports, I beseech thee; and grant me the grace to imitate thy unalterable meekness, in whatever situation I may be placed, and thence to enjoy eternal peace.

One *Pater*, five *Glorias*—O amiable Heart, &c.

V. May thy generous Heart, victorious over death and hell, be honoured with every praise; it merits them all, O my Jesus! As for me, I am more than ever confounded at beholding mine so pusillanimous, that a vain expression or the smallest object alarms it; but it shall be so no more. Grant me strength to combat and to conquer upon earth, to the end that, triumphing over all, I may, with thee, be replenished with joy in heaven.

One *Pater*, five *Glorias*—O amiable Heart, &c.

Let us turn towards Mary, in consecrating ourselves to the Heart of her Son ; and full of confidence in her maternal tenderness, say to her :

BY the fervent prayers of your most meek Heart, obtain for me, O Mary, Mother of God and my mother, a true and constant devotion to the Sacred Heart of Jesus your Son : to the end that, uniting with you in thoughts and affections, I may think only of fulfilling my duties, and of maintaining myself in an interior peace, until that moment when I shall appear before him.

V. Heart of Jesus ! glowing with love for us,

R. Grant that our heart may be inflamed with the love of thee.

Let us pray.

WE beseech thee, O Lord! that the Holy Ghost may enkindle in us that fire which Jesus Christ has drawn from the profundity of his Heart to extend over the earth, and which he desires to see enkindled.   He who liveth and reigneth for ever and ever.   *Amen.*

THE ASSOCIATION OF THE HOLY AND IMMACULATE HEART OF MARY.

THE archconfraternity under this title was established at Paris, in the Church of Notre Dame des Victoires, December 16th, 1836. It was approved by the Pope, April 24th, 1838, with the privilege of aggregating to itself other similar associations. The primary object of the Association is to pray for the conversion of sinners and of persons in error; and God has been pleased to answer its prayers in a most remarkable manner.

All that is absolutely necessary on the part of each associate is, after registration of name, to recite every day the "Hail Mary," for the intentions of the Association. The following pious exercises, though well suited to answer the ends of the Association, are not strictly required—

An Act of Oblation, to be recited Daily.

I OFFER up to God all the thoughts words, and actions of this day, and more particularly all my prayers and devotions, through the Holy and Immaculate Heart of the ever-blessed Virgin Mary ; and I pray for the conversion of sinners, especially those who have been recommended to my prayers, and for the sanctification of all in this community.

Mary, refuge of sinners, pray for us. Mary, conceived without sin, pray for us, who seek thy succour.

Hail Mary, &c.

It is recommended further—1. To communicate once a month ; 2. To recite the rosary once a week ; both for the intentions of the Association ; 3. To wear, as a badge, the medal of the Immaculate Conception ; 4. To say often the " Memorare " prayer.

The Plenary Indulgences granted to the associates, with the usual conditions, are—1. On the day of admission ; 2. At the hour of death ; 3. On the Sunday before Septuagesima, the principal Feast of the Association ; 4. On the Feast of our Lord's Circumcision ; 5. On the Feasts of the Purification, Annunciation, Assumption, Conception, Dolours, and Nativity of Our Blessed

Lady; 6. On the Feast of the Conversion of St. Paul; 7. On the Feast of
St. Mary Magdalen; 8. On any two
days of the month; 9. On the anniver-
sary of their baptism.

There is also an indulgence of 500
days, for all the members and other
persons who assist at the Masses celebrated on Saturdays, in honour of the
Holy and Immaculate Heart of Mary, in
the church or chapel of the Confrater-
nity, and there pray for the conversion
of sinners. The benefits of the Association extend beyond this life; for a
Mass is celebrated for the deceased
members at Notre Dame des Victoires
on the first Saturday of every month.

———o———

Prayer to the Immaculate Heart of Mary.

O HEART of Mary, Mother of God and
our mother, Heart most worthy of
love, object of the complacency of the
most Holy Trinity, and deserving of all
the veneration and tenderness of angels
and of men, thou art most like the
Heart of Jesus, of which thou art the

most perfect image. O Heart full of
goodness and compassion for our
miseries, vouchsafe to thaw the ice of
our hearts, and make them to be entirely turned to the heart of our Divine
Saviour. Pour into them the love of
thy virtues, inflame them with that
blessed fire with which thou continually
burnest, shut up within thyself the
Holy Church, guard it and be always its
sweet asylum and its tower of strength
against all the incursions of its enemies.
Be thou our way to go to Jesus, and
the channel by which we receive all the
graces necessary for our salvation. Be
thou our succour in our wants, our support in our afflictions, our comfort in
temptations, our refuge in persecutions,
our aid in all dangers, but especially
in the last combat of our life at the
hour of death, when all hell will be un-
chained against us to snatch our souls
away in that most dreadful moment, on
which our eternity depends. Oh, then,
most tender Virgin, make us feel the
sweetness of thy maternal Heart, and
the greatness of thy power with the

Heart of Jesus, and open to us in that same fountain of Mercy a secure refuge, that we may come to bless him with thee in Paradise for ever and ever. *Amen.*

May the divine Heart of Jesus and the Immaculate Heart of Mary be known, praised, blessed, loved, served, and glorified, ever and everywhere. *Amen.*

Indulgences—Sixty days, once a day. Plenary, for those who may say it, daily, on the Feasts of our Lady's Nativity, Assumption, and her Heart; provided that after Confession and Communion they visit a church or altar dedicated to her, and pray for the intention of the Sovereign Pontiff. Both are applicable to the dead.

25 FE67